BREATHE, FEEL, HEAL, AWAKEN:

LIVING AND LOVING YOUR HEART'S PATH

By PHILLIP S. MITCHELL,

M.A., MFT, MAC

First Printed Edition, July, 2012

Second Printing, September, 2012

Copyright 2012, Phillip S. Mitchell.

ISBN 13-9781482719147

Author can be contacted at Enheartenment Publishing, *Enheartenment@AOL.com*

~ PRINTED ON RECYCLED PAPER ~

ECPrinting.com - Eau Claire, WI

Yeolus

TABLE OF CONTENTS

Acknowledgements

I wish to express much gratitude to **Amy Levinson** who so graciously helped with this project in many ways. Her beautiful, generous heart, her expertise, her urge to serve and more are a great gift. Thank you, dear Amy.

And to Amy's Dad, **Jay Levinson**, 'Father of Guerilla Marketing' and author of dozens of books on the subject. Jay has frequently urged me over the years to write about what's in me. Thank you, dear Jay.

Much gratitude goes to **Linda Johns**, Animal Communicator, spiritual guide, healer and more. Thank you dear Linda for your wonderful gift of vision and loving guidance all along.

My gratitude to **Yeshua**, my Spirit Guides, Saki, Lisa deLongchamps, Danaan Parry, Virginia Satir, Ram Dass, Bashar, Lazaris, SaLuSa for your awakenings and guidance.

Thank you to the great writers that inspired me: Alan Watts, Dion Fortune, Colin Wilson, Joan Halifax, PhD, Joan Grant, Dr. Carl Jung, Maurice Merleau-Ponty, Dr. Thomas Szasz, Ralph Waldo Emerson, Ken Carey, Dr. Richard Selzer and more.

Thank you to my dear friends who encouraged me to share my writings; Samson Buss, David Kaler, Don Lavender, Dr. Hayward Fox, Jonathan Jaffe.

And to nephews David & Sam Tepper, cousin David Slack, cousin Al Plotkins, sister Shari Mayes, Grandpa George Mitchell, and

Mae & Bob Plotkin.

And to my dear friends of the '1947 Club' - Iasos, Bo B., Richard D., George K., Paul L., Bill Q., George R., Larry R.

And friends, co-workers and clients at Sierra Tucson.

Deep Gratitude to my Animal Companions who so generously, patiently have taught the greatest lessons of all - Unconditional Love.

And deepest gratitude to **Gaia** who so generously and tolerantly sustains us all.

~ **A portion of the proceeds from this book will go to several Animal Welfare and Environmental organizations.** ~

Cover Art: 'Indigo Temple' - A Tierazon Fractal Image by: Phillip S. Mitchell, 2006.

Foreword

I slept and dreamt that life was joy.

I awoke and saw that life was service.

I acted and behold; service was joy.

- **Rabindranath Tagore**

Ancient spiritual teachings, Eastern & Western, were largely studies of human consciousness, just as modern psychology endeavors to be.

As I progressed in my studies and work in these areas, this realization grew. It's all the same business. In the helping professions, the service we provide to our patients and clients is as much spiritual as it is of psychological and emotional healing.

Much of Humanisitic Psychology in the 1960's evolved in the 1970's into what we refer to as Transpersonal Psychology. This brand of psychology constitutes the blending of the spiritual with the psychological, and allows for a deeper and broader scope. Dr. Carl Jung knew this and studied extensively in both worlds. He is often regarded as the _Father of Transpersonal Psychology_.

The proceeding chapters reflect this blending with the intention of informing or reminding readers of some useful, healing connections, often overlooked. This book is intended for spiritual seekers, helping professionals, people engaged in 12-Step Recovery, and more.

As some of the chapters were written as articles for magazines and other publications, there is a measure of repetition of some key themes. My wish is that the reader will benefit in considering these themes from various perspectives and, thus, allow them to deepen.

Mainly, I hope this reading will prove enjoyable, useful and contribute to enhanced service to all - especially at this unique timing, 2012 AD, a time of *profound* change and evolution.

Namaste. - PSM, Oro Valley, AZ, USA, May, 2012

1. EMBRACING EMOTION

Many people on their journey of physical embodiment have shared a concern regarding the various types of spiritual work they've done and why they seem to slip back into old patterns and blockages. With such concerns also comes confusion regarding the importance of emotion; expressing it, transcending it, etc.

Certain tools of understanding have come to me during my career as a spiritually-oriented (Transpersonal) psychotherapist and guide, which you may find them helpful.

The Eastern concept of transcending emotion has often been misinterpreted to mean bypassing or denying our feelings. This couldn't be further from the truth. The Creator didn't err by giving us the circuitry for feeling states. Our emotional body is a crucial part of this physical aspect of our spiritual journey. There is no getting *rid* of feelings, *per se*. There is only getting *through* them and thus learning from them.

Whenever we block or deny our feelings, they intensify and become larger in our experience. Whatever we choose to deny, that object of denial becomes what our life is about in that moment. A part of us will remain busy remembering to deny a feeling or event. We've thus achieved the opposite of what we desired to achieve by our denial; the pile under the carpet becomes larger and we're more likely to trip over it.

The opposite of denial is *acceptance*. With acceptance, we're poised to move with and through the issue or feeling at hand so that we can learn from it and move on to what's next on our path.

It's important to drop self-judgment when we recognize our denial. Remember the time when you taught yourself to deny certain feelings? Often I look to the ages of four to eight when we made crucial pacts with ourselves, often associated with what me may have experienced as trauma or other difficulties. At the time, it was good, creative, intelligent, to do so. It was your survival *then.* To continue that behavior now, however, exacts an increasing price; it drains your precious life energy and keeps you from realizing your wholeness.

The Importance of Honoring Feelings

When feelings are blocked or denied, there are predictable costs and symptoms. The body will faithfully express any number of pathologies, often in areas of the body where the feeling is blocked. As Dr. Chopra has often remarked, *"It's not that the mind is in the body. Rather, the body is in the mind."* Such disorders include tumors, cancers, gastrointestinal problems and heart ailments and more. James Hillman wrote; *"The body is a citadel of metaphor."*

Certain pathologies have been referred to as psychosomatic. Many physicians and healers today concur that among the factors that lead to such conditions are emotional and psychological events that must be addressed before thorough, holistic healing can take place. Many people would include so-called accidents in the same category. Among the various psychological/emotional factors, non-forgiveness of self and/or others plays a crucial part in any pathology.

In relationships, every unexpressed feeling serves as a brick in the wall between parties, creating the opposite of what most of us wish for in a relationship, namely intimacy.

In the area of livelihood, creativity and productivity are sharply compromised when we're not current in sharing feelings.

Fear and Love

Our two basic feeling states are associated with two areas of the body in which they are sourced. The fear feelings (fear, anger, guilt and shame) are sourced in the 'gut' area. We may have symptoms elsewhere (shallow breath or no breath, stiff upper back, shoulders & neck, dry mouth, sweaty palms).

The love feelings (including the range of feelings from sadness to joy, as well as love, compassion and peace) are sourced in the heart area / heart chakra. This is not just the physical heart, but a greater area around the heart. Feelings of loneliness and hurt, which include fear and sadness, draw from both areas in the body.

Imagine a child who grew up in a typically dysfunctional family system learned that feeling or expressing anger was not acceptable. To be accepted by those adults who provided for her, that child taught herself to suppress anger. This was good; her survival mechanism was intact. Her child-self, which is still a part of the adult, needs appreciation, not condemnation, for finding her unique way to survive.

Now, 30 years later, so much of her precious life energy is spent managing/controlling this intensified ball of anger in her gut that it's taking a noticeable toll in her work, relationships and health. It's difficult for her to feel any sense of spiritual connectedness. Perhaps she's become addicted to a harmful substance in an attempt to manage the continuous, gnawing pain of keeping her feelings supressed. It's become increasingly necessary for her to clear this blockage so that she can have and share a life.

She would do well to forgive herself for trying to adapt, in the best way she could as a child, to the rules of her family's system in order be accepted. Dropping her self-judgment, moving through the blockage and allowing herself to feel and release those feelings will move her beyond the stuckness. She can then proceed with her spiritual journey of life.

When any feeling is 'knocking at the door,' it is important to feel and express it freely and fully, as soon as possible. This does not require forcing the feeling or dramatizing it, which is as false as stuffing or denying it. Simply to let it come up and allow it free expression. The following Feeling Formula can be used as a guide in honoring and processing feelings:

1. Feel it, *breathe with it* (literally) and express it as soon as possible, in a non-blaming way.

2. This will release and heal it for the time being. It might be unrealistic to expect 100% clearing of emotion each time - we are not machines. We can, however, release significant amounts of emotional content this way.

3. Steps 1 & 2 prepare us for the learning and growing which automatically occurs when feelings are honored. Evolving is a key reason we chose to be in physical embodiment in this planetary schoolhouse of Earth.

Please note that this process is supported and facilitated by deep and slow breathing. Full breath aligns our many levels of being to allow for fullest release and learning.

I would suggest that there are no negative feelings, although there may be negative or harmful behaviors. Each feeling offers a gift of learning, *faster than the fastest mind can compute*, when allowed to run its course. The clean expression of anger (for example, "When you said that to me the other night, I felt hurt and angry.") has never hurt anyone. Rage, on the other hand, is a learned behavior, not a feeling, and is often used as a way to suppress unacceptable feelings. Rage takes many forms of behavior, from silent to violent. It can hurt others and will inevitably hurt the person expressing it.

Another reminder about fear and the fear feelings: many of us on spiritual paths have judged fear and related feelings negatively, and have avoided feeling or expressing *negative* feelings. Again, the Creator didn't err in providing us with the circuitry for such feelings. When these feelings are present, give yourself total permission to talk about it, get it out, feel it, shake with it, cry with it — whatever it wants to do in its natural expression.

Sometimes simply identifying your greatest fear in any given moment will begin the trickle effect of its own release. If you're not cognizant of its source, process it anyway and trust that the cognitive connection will come in its own time. Although the cognitive connection may come at some point and be helpful, it is not prerequisite to processing the feeling.

Therefore, make no judgments, and do not over-rely on cognitive understanding of your feeling. Simply give yourself total permission to have it and then express it with full, continuous breathing.

One of the great myths of Western culture has been that all knowledge is contained in the gray matter or brain. The human body, including its aura, is actually a field of living intelligence and awareness. If we were to block certain feelings, then most assuredly we'd block the literal, invaluable information that we're wired for.

The fear feelings are concerned with protecting our physical being while we're associated with the body, period. When fear is denied and thus intensified, its residue often winds up in the 'control tower' of the ego-mind, mixing with our thoughts and causing us to believe that everything we experience is scary and requires constant effort to control. All controlling behavior can be seen as a result of unresolved fear and will become uncontrollable unless that underlying fear is acknowledged and released.

Perfectionism is also a type of controlling behavior, borne of a type of unprocessed fear: *shame*, which is fear of being judged.

When we process our fear feelings, it is easier to experience the more subtle love feelings and access our deep, invaluable heart-knowing, which we're all wired for.

The love feelings, when honored, allow us to access our highest and deepest knowing, through the heart center, that most vital conduit or 'telephone to the higher self' or Creator.

To take this understanding a step further, one might ask, "What is the force that animates our emotions?" *Spirit itself.* Therefore, to block emotion is to block spirit energy and spirit-knowing from coursing through your being. What a loss that would be!

Thus far we've been viewing the emotions as a window inward, to knowing and expressing who we are. As we proceed through this critical juncture of accelerated evolution, we'll be reclaiming knowledge of our emotional body that will allow us to vibrate specific feeling centers, using them to attract/create the experiences and realities we prefer, and thus using emotion as a tool of empowerment, of manifestation; a window outward and more.

Embracing the emotional body is an essential part of our spiritual development. The idea is not that we *are* our emotions, any more than we are our thoughts. Yet, we experience emotions and feelings, and by honoring them we learn much. We can learn to move with them more quickly and fully and truly progress along our chosen paths. This choice will honor and accelerate the evolutionary moment that we so courageously chose to engage with at this space/time.

So, breathe. Feel. Release. Know. Let the joy flow and express as that expression of Spirit that you are.

*The Latin *spiritus* means breath/wind, power/energy, as does *ruach* in Hebrew, *pneuma* in Greek, *prana* in Sanscrit, chi in Chinese, and *ki* in Japanese.

2. REDUCING RESISTANCE

"If resistance isn't happening [in some form with the client in therapy], then nothing is happening." - Mary Merrill, PhD, Santa Rosa, CA, 1977

"Resistance is futile."- The Borg (from 'Star Trek')

"What we resist, persists"- Anonymous

How We Learned to Resist Change

Resistance is a product of fear; specifically fear of change. The ego or child self does not differentiate good change from bad and is likely to regard *any* change as a threat to their known existence. It will tend to do anything in its power to thwart or stop change or forward movement, regardless of how much positive change is wanted or needed. Our known sets of circumstances, regardless of how dysfunctional or unpleasant they may be, are *familiar* and therefore afford us the illusion of safety and control. We tend to gravitate toward the familiar, the habitual, that which is within our comfort zone. We seek to preserve our definition of personal safety and well-being that we learned or taught ourselves in childhood.

A baby or child, for example, seeks a stable and secure environment in order to survive and thrive. We learn to rely on our caregivers to provide a non-changing, non-chaotic environment in which our physical, psychological, and spiritual needs our met in a predictable, timely and orderly fashion. Children raised in chaotic home environments with frequent changes may carry ingrained, often repressed fear as does an adult who acts out with anxiety and addiction disorders.

Healthy parents will provide a structure and schedule (without being overly rigid) that a child learns to rely upon. Stability equates with survival in the child's mind.

Upon closer inspection, however, it often becomes clear that often what we believed was safe may be anything but safe. For example, an alcoholic taught himself in his teens that if he drank with his peers he would be assured social acceptance. Indeed, it may appear to 'work' for a time. However, the progressive cost of this behavior, including increasing social, medical, legal, financial and other problems is in direct contrast to what he once believed was true. What was once safe, what assured him social acceptance, is now replaced by mounting cost and danger to one's whole being as well as to others. Even though he learned in childhood that change is a threat to survival, change is now a necessity. The hard-wiring of the brain must be revised.

Normalizing Negative Feelings

Resistance is based upon fear; often unprocessed, repressed or unconscious fear. Fear and its related core feelings of anger, guilt and shame, receive bad press and are referred to as the 'negative' emotions. Every emotion carries instantaneous information that we'd do well to listen to and honor. In that light, it behooves us to to release the limiting judgment that such feelings are 'negative'.

We are given the circuitry for these feelings on purpose, not by mistake. Whether you believe that a Creator gave you feelings, and/or you understand that human biology is wired for survival and the fear-based feelings are your brain's way of providing you cues to help you survive.

The purpose of fear (which goes by many names; anxiety, nervousness, anticipation, worry, etc.) is to protect our physical being while we are associated with physical form. As with any emotion, we benefit from embracing and honoring it, literally breathing with it, listening to its message and then moving on, more informed and aware. This is called "processing your feelings."

16

What should we do with the feeling of fear?

Refrain from judgment about having fear. It's a natural feeling at those times when our physical vehicle perceives threat in some way. When you spend time judging your feelings, the effect of this is the slowing or blocking of gaining the information contained within that feeling. Dealing with the fear that brings forth the resistance and allows for forward movement in our lives.

Next time you feel fear, sit down.

- Feel the feeling and breathe with it.

- Don't try to understand or analyze (where did it come from, why did it happen, what did I do, what can I do, etc.)

- Don't judge it ("This is a bad feeling; I shouldn't be feeling this way.", etc.)

- Do some deep and slow breathing, allowing yourself to shift gears.

- Listen for a 'hit' or intuitive message without analyzing it.

- Move on with eyes open wider.

In the process of change, recovery and growth, we may take three steps forward and two steps back. We move toward a desired goal, which may be movement out of our comfort zone, and the ego may want to pull us back into the perceived comfort zone, regardless of how unsatisfactory, limiting or miserable it may be. This is similar to having one foot on the gas pedal in your car, and one foot on the brake at the same time. Realize that the most important predictor of successful change is *progress, not perfection.*

Another useful metaphor for this process is imagining one's foot nailed into the floor. In such a predicament, all one can do is walk around in the same circle. The territory of the prescribed circle becomes quite familiar after a time; one's comfort zone, however unpleasant or limiting it may be. To remove the nail might be uncomfortable, painful and scary. When it is removed, one has the option of exploring new territory in life, learning and growing. The options of (1) remaining trapped in that circle for another few years of one's gift of life, or (2) removing the nail and walking differently may both be scary. However, the key question is which option is *more* scary. Consider this the next time you have an important decision to make that may pull you out of your comfort zone.

Transformation is a key term for change. Some of us fear that term as well. It is interesting to note, that in the wisdom of Native American teachings, transformation is the most *natural* phenomenon in all of creation.

Other spiritual teachings remind us that we are designed to face and deal with the challenges that we meet or attract. Take a moment now. Visualize a sign-up sheet that you signed up for. It's called "Your Life." It comes with a full curriculum for your soul, now in contract form. Time spent judging your life in this planetary school house takes away from time for learning, growing and transforming—the end result of your soul's contract.

If we're willing to embrace it as such, not fight it, you may even learn to 'enjoy the ride' as you move through your life.

The 'Hows' of Change

If we are willing to allow or accept the next challenge that presents itself to us, without judging it or ourselves, we are in a more favorable position to deal with it, learn from it and proceed with life. Imposing judgment - usually rooted in fear - keeps us locked within a dilemma. We might believe that there's no way out and assume the posture of victimhood. You may have heard the idea that "There are no victims - there are only volunteers." Victimhood is often a choice, not a requirement. Those who assume a victim role get their needs met in an indirect or unhealthy manner. The price tag, especially over time, is tragic.

Allowing and Acceptance are other important terms to understand. If we remember and are willing to allow or accept the next challenge that presents itself to us, without judging it or ourselves for attracting it, we are in a more favorable position to deal with it, learn from it and proceed with life. Imposing typical fear-based judgment on the other hand, has the effect of keeping us locked within that dilemma. We might believe that there's no way out and assume the posture of victimhood. That's an option, a choice. From a common spiritual perspective, this might require forgetting that on a deeper level of being, we 'signed up' for this life, including its full curriculum. We are designed to face and deal with the challenges that we meet or attract. (*'Challatunities'*, I like to call them.)

I'm reminded of the Rider-Waite Tarot card for the Hebrew letter *Ayin*. There is an image of two people chained to the devil's throne, symbolic of material bondage. If you look closely, the chains around their necks are larger than their heads. All they have to do is notice that, lift the chains off and experience freedom. How this so often reflects our own experiences of bondage and self-imposed limitation!

Trust is another term worth exploring a bit further. Many of us often feel that trusting is quite difficult. A spiritual teacher, Bashar, points out that trusting is another very natural phenomenon and that we're always trusting in something. "The question is; do we choose to trust in a positive reality or a negative one?" To paraphrase Frederich Nietzsche and Carlos Casteneda's character, Don Juan Matus; *'There are no facts. There is only interpretation.'*

Sometimes our 'fact' is really a 'fict' - a fear-based projection sourced in our historic perception. When we become aware of that projective mechanism, we are more empowered to catch it and let it rest. Then, with fresher eyes, we can see more clearly, inside and outside of ourselves, without imposing the cataract of past belief. It is easier to trust or choose to trust in our reality and its inhabitants, and give life more of a fair chance.

Are we willing to trust in the essential design of our being enough to welcome and embrace that which seems to put us to the test? We have choice here too; we can fight our experience from the position of fear and victimhood, or we can assume ownership of the experiences that present themselves to us and trust in our implicit ability to engage with them.

Too often, especially in the victim state, we frame our options in terms of ability - "I'm able or unable to do this." It is more honest, accurate and empowering to view, our options can be in terms of what we're *willing* to do. Then we remember we have choice and we're empowered to make healthy choices.

In spiritual study circles, it's often said, "If God brings us *to* it, He will bring us *through* it." To paraphrase Carl Jung: 'Implicit in any dilemma which presents itself to us is our ability to deal with it.' In other words, it's helpful to know that the dilemma wouldn't arise in our experience unless we were capable of meeting it. If you are given the shoes, it's up to you to do the footwork. Change and transformation are not spectator sports; they require active participation in one's own life.

Our choices and beliefs are magnets that attract like experience. *We are the creators and co-creators that the Creator created.* We have our part in attracting our experiences.

The Outcome of Accepting Change

When we are awake, more conscious of our inner processes, tendencies and fears, we're poised to catch ourselves judging, over-analyzing, playing the victim or not trusting. We have the innate ability to make healthier, new decisions once we get out of our own way.

As we 'catch' ourselves using the survival tactics that we learned in childhood to prevent change, it is important to refrain from self-condemnation. Instead of thinking to yourself, "Darn, there I go again!" Ask yourself: "What would I *prefer* to do differently this time in order to feel better about myself and learn something new?" Lisa deLongchamps, a wonderful spiritual teacher, would often remind her students that in our decision-making, the question of the victim is "What do I *need*?" And the voice of the master is "What would I *prefer*?"

Deep and slow breathing at this juncture has the effect of inserting a 'crowbar' into the machinery of old habits. Deep breathing makes it easier to catch oneself and effectively establish healthy change. Readily forgive yourself if the new behavior doesn't seem to immediately work well in your estimation. Give yourself a reasonable time-frame to establish fresh ways of operating.

With practice, we can teach ourselves that we needn't necessarily fear or resist healthy, natural change that wants to occur and enrich our lives. We learn that it's safe to go forward at a pace that we can assimilate. We learn that it's safe to have a life outside of the confines or prisons of belief with which we have heretofore bound ourselves.

3. SHAME REDUCTION AND DESERVABILITY

"Repentance is a doorway, not an abode; it is of value only when it inspires healthy change and passes on into a state of restored self-acceptance. To value yourself less than God values you is not humility, it is pride of a most destructive nature."

- Ken Carey, The Third Millennium, Harper Collins, 1991, p. 154

[*Deservability* is a term coined by the late Lisa de Longchamps, founder of the former Wingsong School in Oakland, CA which operated from the mid-1970's to the early 1990's. This chapter is dedicated to Lisa, her 'laser-beam' teachings, her indomitable spirit and her message of joy as the natural state of being. Several of the concepts offered here were conveyed by Lisa during her various workshops.]

Deservability refers to the willingness to accept love in our lives in its myriad forms. Unresolved shame, as with guilt and other forms of fear, can interfere with one's acceptance of that which is good in life. You may ask, but what is shame exactly? Shame is fear of being judged by others; fear associated with one's identity; fear of being rejected by family or others. Guilt is vibrationally* very close to shame. It pertains to behavior and it is the fear of being punished for something you've done.

Guilt and shame are subject to healthy and toxic states. In a *healthy* state, when we feel guilt and shame, we honor these feelings as they arise, learn from them and move on.

All emotional states carry with them instantaneous information that we'd do well to embrace and learn from. In this light, there are no "negative feelings", although there certainly have been many negative or destructive behaviors associated with the suppression, inflation or other means of dishonoring or distorting our natural feelings or emotions. Healthy guilt and shame describe one's core values and help us identify acceptable modes of behavior for ourselves.

When these feelings arise, we benefit from listening to their messages without judgment and 'trimming our sails' accordingly.

Toxic guilt and shame have to do with tendencies to punish ourselves; going far beyond listening to the feeling and modifying our behavior. No one is served when we get busy 'beating ourselves up' with toxic levels of these feelings. Feelings that are toxic become exaggerated when either denied or expressed in a manner beyond what is necessary.

In the toxic condition, we may believe that we *are* our guilt or shame.

These understandings may serve in creating a foundation or method for the working through, learning from, and releasing/ healing these feelings. Patience with self and others in allowing adequate processing time is crucial. Healthy processing of feelings may include:

1 Letting yourself feel the emotion without judging it; literally breathing with the feeling as it comes

2 Using clear, non-abusive communication with others as needed

3 Expressive anger release in a manner that hurts no one or no thing

4 Reflecting on the experience and the lessons learned by writing in your journal or discussing it with a friend, therapist or other objective listener.

Frequently, as we process old shaming messages that we have accepted, we may begin to realize that these messages did not really pertain to us; they were the inter-generational 'hot potatoes' of abusive communication or behavior passed on to us, sometimes simply because we were a vulnerable recipient who was there. As a recipient of such shaming messages, we have the opportunity to clear them or break the cycle, rather than continue their passage onto another.

As we reduce the excess shame that we've been carrying, our 'cup' is less full of shame-based content and now has room to hold another kind of substance. There is now room to hold new levels of self-worth and love in its many forms. As we learn to fill our cups with this new substance, we are naturally more capable of sharing that which we own with others, including those we love.

No human is perfect. Perfectionism is a product of unprocessed, usually toxic, shame. The attempt to produce 'perfect' behaviors is often fueled by the illusion that "If I look good and do everything perfectly, then others won't judge me as I judge myself." Of course, this demand is impossible to maintain in our humanness and will be very frustrating for the individual and for those involved with him or her.

We can practice **self-forgiveness** every day and not overdo it. We can forgive ourselves for not conforming to our own idea of perfection and for other issues if we are willing, and thus prepare our cup to receive the love that's aching to enter our lives. We may also choose to strive for excellence in what we do if we'd like, and recognize the distinction between excellence and perfectionism.

As noted above, perfectionism is an unhealthy or pathological condition. Striving for excellence in your chosen area of interest is healthy, often a wonderful, enriching pursuit for you and others.

Another most powerful tool for replacing shame with a healthy sense of self-worth and confidence is found in choosing to behave impeccably. Lisa defined **impeccability** (not to be confused with perfectionism) as follows: *"The conscious choice to operate from the highest level of awareness that you've attained, and to do this as consistently as humanly possible."* A simple shortcut to

24

identify your impeccable behavior is to ask yourself; "What is the most *loving* thing that I can do or say, or not do / not say, in a particular situation?" (Codependents be advised: you must include yourself in the equation of determining the most loving thing or the *greatest good* for all in any such situation.) You will notice that this question will instantly provide you with access to the highest level of awareness available to you.

When we choose to operate with such impeccability frequently, over time, our self-esteem and sense of deservability can only increase. Our cup begins to overflow with endless forms of love that we can share effortlessly with our world. With practice, we become more attuned to rapidly identifying the greatest good to pursue in most situations.

For example, a codependent person simply refrains from doing their habitual caretaking behaviors, which may be more of a nuisance to others than a real benefit. That simple refraining from acting on the patterned impulse would constitute impeccability in that situation. And, of course, there are myriad other examples of impeccability involving actions that clearly benefit others.

To keep the good from leaving our cup prematurely, a bottom to the cup is necessary. **Healthy boundaries**** constitute the bottom of our cup. Communicating with clear, healthy boundaries informs others, and our own bio-computers, that we are worthy of respectful treatment and love.

Lastly, our willingness to feel **gratitude** is most important. Feeling gratitude for your ability and willingness to allow your life to improve and for the gifts that you receive will attract more love. As Lisa would often remind us, "Complaint creates a mold which will attract more to complain about. Gratitude creates a different kind of mold which will attract more to be grateful for." We certainly have our part in the co-creation of what we experience.

May this formula work well for you, as it does for me and so many of my friends and clients.

"The possible becomes probable through the mysterious alchemy of self-love and joyous expectation. The probable becomes reality through the willingness to receive." - Lazaris

* Many emotions and states of mind can be measured in vibrational frequency with bio-feedback and similar devices. Guilt and shame are very close in vibration as fear-related feelings, just as forgiveness and gratitude are 'sister vibrations' of love-based or heart-centered feelings.

** From **Boundaries: Tools of Respect**, an article by Phillip S. Mitchell, 'Addiction Professional' magazine, Jan., 2004.

4. CODEPENDENCY: A DIALOG

"How empty of me to be so full of you."- Cyndi Collier, Therapist

"What you think of me is none of my business." - Terry Cole-Whitaker, Author, Teacher

Questioner: "So what's all this fuss about codependency? What is it, really?"

Answerer: "Well, to begin, there is an outdated definition that's still floating about, that may muddy the waters. Until the 1970's, it was usually a term used to define the enabling relationship of a spouse toward an addicted partner. Frequently, a wife toward an alcoholic husband. 'Enabling' is a term for the refusal to confront another's unacceptable behavior.

"Since the late 1970's, it has been generally recognized that codependency expresses itself through many styles or roles, not just that of the enabler. Other roles include Controller, Caretaker, Fixer, Mediator, People-Pleaser, Martyr, Victim, and the addicted person as well. There are overlaps in some of these role titles, yet they describe variant expressions of codependency. It's important to bear in mind that each role is a product of unresolved fear, mainly fear of non-acceptance or rejection. (More on this below.)

To take this a step further, unresolved fear tends to flow to the 'control tower'; the brain. Then it mixes with our thoughts and expresses as controlling behavior in some form, usually through one or more of the roles just mentioned. As that unresolved fear inhabits body and mind, nearly everything that we perceive outside of ourselves seems to be something to fear. We feel we must maintain control of reality, which is not only exhausting, but impossible. We feel we must control or manipulate others to ensure our needs will be met, versus trusting in others, trusting in life and relaxing into life. The very styles of controlling behaviors that we select are any combination of the codependent roles. The key lesson here for codependents is to recognize that it's not our job to control others. It is our job to manage our own behaviors. When we attempt to control others, we become fatigued, out-of-balance, triggered into any number of self-destructive behaviors, and/or addictions, and solidly in the zone of the victim.

All of the codependent role titles can be seen as variations of the Controller role. When we are functioning in the Controller role, one is taking charge of things and is usually quite up-front about it. The other role titles are simply different styles of controlling behavior. When we have resolved personal fear issues, particularly fear of rejection, there is less fearful residue that finds its way to the control tower. It becomes easier to trust in the world, without the need or compulsion to control situations or other people."

To further clarify the difference between codependence & healthy interdependence, consider the codependent making decisions from fear, specifically fear of rejection. What may appear to be a kind act or gift from this position really is not a gift - there's an expectation that you will then support or accept me, which incurs a price tag for giver and receiver. Its important to examine your motives; what the cost is to you, and what kind of payoff you expect in return. Often the perceived payoff is the expectation that you will be accepted. The others will be 'in your corner' and support you.

Alternatively, if you give a gift or act of kindness from the heart, where it is your joy to do so, that is indeed a gift to both parties simultaneously - and a great example of healthy interdependence.

Q. "Where do codependent behaviors originate?"

A. "Typically, between the ages of 4 & 8 years (but not limited to that age group), a child learns that certain behaviors are approved of or supported by their parents or guardians and some behaviors are not. The child may similarly perceive that he or she is supported or not. Specifically, the parents may or may not give loving attention or show affection for the child. Equally, youngsters need attention to reinforce their identity - to know that they exist and that they're important. Growing up, we know that those big people are our support system and we must please them in some way to ensure continued attention and support, so a child teaches himself to foster certain behaviors and curtail or omit others.

So, we learn early to defer to others and select behaviors that 'work' for us. Young children already learn to negate the importance of their own impulses, drives, and preferences. They want to please the big people to ensure their survival. In cases where there's a lack of positive attention, he or she may learn to act out in ways that seem negative if that's what seems to 'work' in gaining attention. One way or the other, we craft ways of ensuring attention. 'Attention = Support = Survival' seems to typify the *m.o.*"

Q. "Isn't everyone codependent in some way? Can't there be a healthy codependency?"

A. "According to some statistics, 96% of our Western culture is codependent. Our innate *interdependence* is a healthy thing to recognize - we are all inextricably connected on a deep level as well as in more apparent ways. To recognize this is healthy and useful. No one can do much alone. Even the most independent innovators or 'self-made' individuals have had someone to help them in some way at every turn.

Codependency, on the other hand, is not healthy by definition. It is a cultural illness or pathology."

Q. "What is the basic definition of codependency?"

A. "There are a few ways to say it. My definition is - *'The compulsive deferring to others to determine what one will say or do.'*

29

'Compulsive', meaning it's hard to stop. Deferring to others is characteristically what one does when we become used to disregarding or distrusting our own feelings. Similar disregard for related intuition and knowing in our decision-making applies here as well. This relates, in turn, to a common cultural taboo of acknowledging and/or expressing feelings, emotion.

In <u>Understanding Co-dependency</u> by Sharon Wegscheider-Cruse, co-dependency is described as "a specific condition that is characterized by preoccupation and extreme dependence — emotionally, socially and sometimes physically — on a person or object. Eventually, this dependency on another person or object becomes a pathological condition that affects the co-dependent in all other relationships"

If we remain in the habit of suppressing our feelings in order to follow our conception of being acceptable to others (or any other reason), we pay a penalty. This penalty includes our being disconnected to our true selves, our core being.

Q. "What are the 'core feelings'?"

A. "Our core feelings/emotions include fear, anger guilt, shame, sadness, love, joy, gratitude, peace. Other terms may apply, but they can usually be ascribed to one or more of these feelings.

Each feeling carries with it *literal information* from our inner or core selves to our more common, everyday awareness. Each feeling state carries with it useful information from our core being outward. To identify certain feelings as 'negative' is to pass unfair and shallow judgment on the emotion and to miss the point. There are no 'negative feelings', although there certainly can be negative expressions of feelings or hurtful behaviors.

Also, we needn't fear our feelings, as many of us have been taught. We are designed to have and express feelings. Therefore, they're inherently safe.

Q. "So what do core feelings have to do with codependency?"

A. "Good question! They have much to do with codependency.

Not honoring one's core feelings is a symptom of codependency as much as it is a result of it. When we feel so compelled to override our core feelings, and equally our core values, in order to experience a sense of acceptance by certain others, we have cancelled out a sense of self. When operating in this cut-off manner consistently, over time, we tend to feel a growing emptiness inside and a greater need to follow the ways of others. This personal disenfranchisement is its own self-perpetuating mechanism.

In the disconnected state, one has forfeited their 'life rudder' or navigation system. The resulting emptiness or void increases, often contributing to the experience of depression and anxiety. In such a state, the codependent person becomes more inclined to look outside of themselves for fulfillment. This out-sourced fulfillment may take the form of an exaggerated need to be valued by others; a 'people addiction'. Other addictive or self-destructive behaviors may equally arise in attempt to fill the void.

Also, in the perennially disconnected state, we may feel more inclined to want to form a primary relationship. If we do so, we are likely to attract another on a similar vibrational level with similar codependent neediness. As in physics, like attracts like. What is likely to occur is a pseudo-relationship where neither party is connected or operating from their authentic self. The avoidance of knowing *self* is doubled and two parties are now interacting without authenticity; not knowing themselves, much less the other.

Disconnect from one's feelings and the subsequent inability to share one's feelings prevents any real intimacy.

Any relationship at that stage is better referred to as an *entanglement*. Here, each party responds to a fear-based, projected image of the other partner, ever trying to please / be accepted by the other according to unresolved history. The series of such entanglements tends to be quite predictable with repeated drama, and ultimately quite boring as well. Neither party shares true intimacy and neither party evolves. 'Complete or repeat' seems to be the rule."

Q. "What are the codependent roles we play?"

A. "The common roles are:

Controller - The person who tends to takes charge of everyone's lives. In the workplace, if ones postion is that of supervisor in some capacity, it's her job to be a leader and director. If she doesn't know how to take off that hat when she comes home, that's a problem. It is not desirable or healthy to manage people in family or other social relationships. The exception is raising children. It's the parent's or guardian's job to provide direction, rules, guidelines and such for children - and hopefully to do that in a balanced, loving way; respectful of each unique soul.

Controlling behavior outside the workplace can be intrusive, disrespectful. Again, such controlling is the product of unresolved fear. The unresolved fear tends to influence the 'control tower' / the brain, and everything observed in one's domain seems to be fearful & must be controlled. As the Controller learns to process and release historic fears, there's less impetus to attempt to control others and more of a willingness to trust in others and in the Universe.

Caretaker/Fixer - There is some overlap in these role titles, yet they have value in identifying key roles. Caretakers and fixers are ever attending to others needs, often overlooking their own. They are exercising controlling behaviors through the guise of being helpful to others. However, this helpfulness is often more of an invasion in another's space, versus true assistance. Equally, it reflects a lack of healthy interpersonal boundaries - it objectifies others and is therefore disrespectful.

People Pleaser - These folks take caretaking to another level, ever-attempting to please in order to gain another's favor. The behavior may *look* nice, but it has as much of a hook of expectation from another as the other codependent roles. Pleasers often aggregate much cumulative, suppressed anger which can 'eat them up' in various ways, as well as explode harmfully at times.

Enabler/Rescuer - The enabler does not confront another's unacceptable behaviors, such as a spouse or partner who is active in their addiction. Fear of rejection or abandonment is usually the driving force once again. The rescuer may be taking that behavior to the next level and the offender in the relationship does not have to take responsibility for their unhealthy behaviors. In a bigger picture, it's not a gift to another to prevent them facing the consequences, and thus learning from, their own behaviors. Their growth is thwarted. There's a common saying in group therapy settings; 'The *rescued* need *rescue* from the *rescuer*.' Or - 'Help! I'm being rescued!!'

Mediator - Mediators tend to have little tolerance for conflict around them. They probably learned in their family of origin how to step into the middle of conflict and make peace between warring factions. It's no secret that many of us in the helping professions learned to be good little mediators, often caretakers too, to survive during childhood.

Martyr - The *song* of the martyr is *'Look at all I've done for you!'* Often referred to as a *guilt-trip*. A very effective way to manipulate others to do for you - if they bite that hook.

Victim - The *song* of the victim is usually *'Why do bad things always happen to me??'* Notice how quickly victims get their needs met, especially by a caretaker or enabler who might not see through the ruse. It appears that the victim, along with the other codependent roles, gets certain needs met. But it is in an unhealthy, indirect manner that winds up costing them their very sense of self.

A key to understanding all of these codependent roles is to see them as variations of the basic *Controller* role - fueled by unresolved fear, objectifying others and manipulating them to meet your needs and desires. Just as all of these roles begin in *Controller*, they end up in *Victim*. When one lives a life deferring to others and learning how to manipulate others, they are not attending to their true selves or core values. Over time, an emptiness or void grows inside and they become a victim of their own behavioral choices. That emptiness may be defined as depression and/or anxiety and they might become more inclined to engage in self-destructive behaviors such as substance abuse or behavioral addictions."

Q. "Does all of this imply that we're not supposed to do nice things for others anymore?"

A. "This is where it's important to know and to trust your feelings. If you're coming from typical codependent fear of rejection, when doing an act of kindness for another, there's an expectation that you get something back from the other, *i.e.* their acceptance of you. This is not a gift or true kindness for wither party.

If, on the other hand, you're coming from feelings such as love and joy in your heart; 'It would be my true *pleasure* to do this for her.', then do it. That will surely be a gift to you and to the recipient simultaneously."

Q. "Okay, so how do we get out of all this stuckness?"

A. "First, just *see* it - whatever role or combination of roles may be active in yourself. Don't judge yourself for it. Remember - that's how you taught yourself to survive in a challenging situation way back when. You did the best you could *then*, given the hand that you were dealt (or dealt yourself; however you prefer to understand this). Therefore, self-judgment is irrelevant at best and impedes your clear view of your behaviors.

Then, breathe deeply, slowly, continuously. That effectively inserts a *crowbar* into the machinery of your awareness and will 'stop the movie' sufficiently to ask yourself; 'How would I *prefer* to respond in this familiar scenario in order to feel better about myself? Then act on that new impulse. Do the best you can - it doesn't have to be 'perfect'. "Practice, nor perfection', as is commonly said. Then, with your eyes open wider to such awareness, and with practice and support from others, you can gradually learn to *steer your ship* in a healthier, more authentic direction.

5. BOUNDARIES: TOOLS OF RESPECT

"Good fences make good neighbors." ~Robert Frost

One of the commonalities of codependent behaviors is the lack of healthy personal boundaries. With various types of dysfunction within our families of origin, there was often a lack of respect shown in personal interactions, including various forms of abuse; physical, sexual, mental, emotional, and spiritual. Implicit in any form of abuse is the message to the victims that they are abusable, worthless, and certainly unworthy of having personal boundaries. This scenario is equally at the root of shame.

Examples of a lack of boundaries include but are not limited to:

- A poor sense or disregard of personal space-not sensing or knowing how physically close you should be in relation to another

- Sharing too much personal information with someone you don't know well

- Falling in love with a new acquaintance

- Obsessive thinking about another person

- Acting on the first sexual impulse

- Being sexual for your partner and not yourself

- Disregarding your personal values in order to please others

- Ignoring another person's display of poor boundaries or invasion of your boundaries

- Accepting food, gifts, touch, or sex that you don't want

- Excessive giving or taking

- Letting others describe you or your reality

- Expecting others to anticipate and fulfill your needs

- Manipulative behaviors, abusive behaviors, etc.

One of the effects of a lack of boundaries is the impaired ability to discern the difference in identity between self and another. Many codependent people do not know where they end and someone else begins. This may express as enmeshment with another, where you may adopt thoughts and feelings of another person and any semblance of boundaries is blurred, if not altogether lost. In extreme forms, this may be referred to as symbiosis, to borrow a term from biology. It is difficult to develop a healthy relationship with enmeshment present. Healthy boundaries can be an important part of the healing of such a dilemma.

Codependent people, for example, perhaps in the roles of Caretaker, Fixer, or People-Pleaser, may appear to be highly focused on another person and very sensitive to that person's needs, yet they are in many ways, unaware of the other's deeper needs or essence. This is because codependents are involved in projecting their imagined beliefs about that person onto him or her, often unconsciously, based upon their own unresolved fear from past experiences. This is usually a fear of non-acceptance, rejection, or abandonment.

Addicts, especially while under the influence of a drug of choice, also tend to demonstrate a lack of healthy boundaries. Many of their sensibilities and sensitivities become increasingly blunted or impaired, and they are likely to become incapable of knowing the true needs and desires of another.

Many of those in recovery find that certain therapeutic tools, recovery activities, and spiritual pursuits aid in establishing or restoring healthy boundaries. As important as this is, it's equally important to learn and practice healthy styles of communication. Even the closest or healthiest relationships require that clear, verbal boundaries be expressed from time to time. Leaving boundaries simply to assumption in a relationship is not always sufficient.

Sometimes a boundary can be as simple as saying "No," which is a complete communication of its own. At other times, some elaboration is needed.

It is important to note that a boundary is *not a threat*. Threats are antiquated, fear-motivated behaviors directed toward changing or 'fixing' another person - another myth of codependence. Such behaviors can only backfire in unpleasant or hurtful ways for both parties. A clean, healthy boundary is a way to inform others as to how you wish to be treated, respected, and loved.

A simple way to set a boundary is to use and practice the following verbal boundary format:

"If you (behavior), I'll share my feelings with you.

If you continue, I'll (action) to take care of myself."

Let's take a closer look at this format and its uses. The first sentence in this format is the assertion of your right or healthy decision to confront unacceptable behaviors in another. Failure to confront such behaviors is *enabling*, or giving another person tacit approval to disrespect or abuse you. Enabling behaviors are driven by the fear of rejection, in some form. A clean confrontation to address unacceptable behavior would be: "When you (behavior), like the time (example), I felt (core feelings)." Notice that this is based simply upon reporting your perception of another's behavior, and your core feelings associated with it. Then, a big PERIOD follows, keeping the communication free of judgment, opinion, shoulds, over-explaining, or lecturing. (It is important to note that the feelings are preceded by "I feel / felt...," - not "you made me feel...," the latter having highly codependent implications.) As with boundaries, the spirit of such a confrontation is to "let the chips fall where they may" versus being invested in a certain outcome pertaining to the other's behavior. The expectation of a certain outcome is likely to be a form of manipulation; another mutually destructive, codependent behavior.

The second sentence of the boundary format is intended to inform (not to punish or threaten) the other of your intended response to their unacceptable behavior if it persists. Whichever action you choose, be sure that it will be sufficient in taking care of yourself in such a situation, and that it's an action that you are willing to commit to, so that your words have meaning. It is also important to select a *minimum muscle* approach to the action statement of a boundary, as, once again, it is not intended as a threat or punishment.

The phrase "to take care of myself" is included to make the entire communication in order to be very explicit about its purpose.

Example: **"If you raise your voice angrily on the telephone with me, I'll share my feelings with you. If you continue, I'll hang up and will not speak to you for two days, to take care of myself."**

Notice that a timeframe is included in the second sentence - two days in this case. Two days might be adequate for taking care of yourself in such an instance, and the other person is unlikely to get the message that the relationship has ended. If the person repeats the behavior, you may wish to repeat the boundary once or twice, raising the ante of the action each time to help them understand, not to punish. If the person continues to disrespect your boundary, a word for that would be abuse - and that's when it's important to remember that no one is served when you allow that part of Spirit that you are to be abused or victimized. That's why your Higher Power gave you those appendages at the end of your legs that make you portable!

Within the scope of healthy boundaries, we are free to experience deeper and safer intimacy in a relationship. We may also clarify when it may be time to end a relationship, or something between these polarities.

Frequent questions that arise in the practice of boundaries are:

Q. "Boundaries seem cold and uncaring. Are we supposed to become uncaring people in using this tool?"

A. No. Boundaries can actually pave the way for greater intimacy, if desired. When we take better care of ourselves with such tools, we actually allow our own cups to become more full, and it is from that position that we have the most to offer in any relationship-not by caretaking another person, but by being more authentic in who we really are and what we wish to express and share with others. Boundaries can be seen as 'the bottom of our cups', allowing various forms of love or goodness to remain in our cups from which we may share.

Q. "What is the difference between having healthy boundaries or having walls built around you?"

A. A person who has constructed walls or barriers around her- or himself is in some degree of isolation from others. Such a person is not available for sharing love in relationship with others. Healthy boundaries, on the other hand, can be flexible, permeable or adaptable for experiencing various degrees of relationship with those you choose, in ways that you choose.

Q. "Many spiritual teachings, including the 12 Steps, teach us that we are interdependent (not having to be codependent) beings, and we are ultimately connected with all life forms. How does this understanding compute with the setting of boundaries in our relationships?"

A. Yes, we are all connected in a very real way. However, it is up to us to responsibly tend to protecting and stewarding the life-form that we represent. With such tools as healthy boundaries, when needed, we are in a position to offer the best of ourselves to all life.

Taking care of ourselves as best we can will support each of us in best serving the Whole, of which we are a part. Conversely, when the Whole is served, we are all served.

6. Alternate Views of Depression

The disciple asks the Master; "How long must I remain in the darkness?"

The Master replies; "Until you learn to see in the darkness."

Depression can be devastating for one who feels locked into that state, as well as for their loved ones who feel powerless in helping them.

Depression is *not* a feeling or emotion. Rather it is a *condition* that often results from emotions and beliefs that may be 'stuck' in one's system.

We are presently emerging from a culture that has taught us to fear our emotions with the assumption that nature was in error when designing humans and other beings with the circuitry for several emotions. We have learned to repress them, ever fearful of their expression. Media bombards us with messages that any emotional state that varies from the 'norm', however that may be defined, is an illness that must be medicated. Many of us have been taught that sadness and crying are forms of weakness; that anger is a most unaceptable emotion to feel or express; that guilt or shame may cripple you; even that too much joy is unrealistic. These cultural misbeliefs do not take into account that there is healing and literal information contained in every emotional state if we are willing to allow their healthy expression.

I would suggest that even the healthy, honest expression of anger has never hurt anyone. The unhealthy expression of it, of course, can be hurtful, destructive. Rage, for example, is not a feeling - it is a learned behavior, from silent to violent. It is often destructive for the one experiencing it as well as those near them. Rage, like depression, is usually the result of other feelings such as anger, fear, shame, guilt, not having healthy expression. The repressed feelings build like steam and seek release. If one has observed rage in another, especially repeatedly during childhood for example, the distorted pathway of rage may be the quickest to come to mind and find such expression. The problem, however, is that rageful behavior will only compound the hurt, and the unexpressed emotions behind it are increased; not released. Not to mention the unfortunate results of rage which will likely return to the rager in some form, at some time.

In learning to to trust one's feelings, one can experience them without the typical fear of having them, and learn that it's ok - even beneficial to do so. Simply *breathing with* an emotion as it arises can aid in embracing it sufficiently to learn that it is inherently safe to feel, release the energy that the emoting is designed to do, and gain necessary insight as to what may be a message from inner self to outer self.

When we experience loss - loss of a loved one through death, or "little deaths" as Dr. Kubler-Ross would say, such as loss of a job, a geographical move, the ending of an important relationship, loss of a physical attribute through an accident, disease or aging, etc. - there is a grieving process that is to be honored. When an emotional attachment is suddenly limited or terminated, the resultant feelings must be felt, aired, released as effectively as possible, and as close in time to the event as possible. Often, this can be done with a therapist, counselor, psychologist or another healing professional. Certain therapeutic techniques could be helpful, such as EMDR, Emotional Field Therapy (EFT) or many other approaches. Sometimes the airing can be done with a good friend or relative willing to listen without trying to 'fix' the grieving person. Such a commitment to emotional self-care will assist the element of time in doing what it can naturally do for us in distancing us from the grieved event and restoring emotional equilibrium in our grieving/ healing process.

"None of us have enough information... to be pessimists." - **Wayne Dyer, PhD.**

If someone is busy loading beliefs reflective of negativity, pessimism, cynicism and such into their bio-circuitry, one would do well to ask; "For what purpose am I doing this?" There is always a purpose - we do nothing without purpose. In simple terms, the purpose is tied one of two motivators; to find pleasure and to avoid pain.

One may have learned that historically in one's life, he or she has not felt thet their needs or desires have been met. In responseto this pattern, they may have made a pact with themselves to *never* let thus & such happen in their lives again. They establish a lifestyle of a certain avoidance that prevents them from allowing for different experiences, learning, expansion, growth. They forcibly keep themselves in a narrow framework which provides the illusion of safety and control. They become completely familiar with the prescribed territory.

For example, someone feels hurt in a significant love relationship and carries forward the fear of being alone. Perhaps this has occurred repeatedly. They make a pact with themselves to never allow for such closeness again in relationships. So, they create and re-create what they most fear - they don't allow for the closeness that they so desire and perpetuate the loneliness they fear.

Such fixed thought and behavior patterns are often at the root of the condition of depression. This is especially true as, over time, one clings to their belief in the necessity of maintaining the earlier pact.

During a psychopathology course in my graduate studies in the late 1970's, my colleagues and I began to worry that we had many of the pathologies to varying degrees that we were studying. This is not an uncommon phenomenon for students in such classes.

43

I went to sleep late one night after studying clinical depression and the subject remained on my mind as I drifted to sleep. Sometimes I get gifts in dreams - insights, jokes, poems, songs, etc. - and I love that. The next morning I awoke with a play on the word 'depressed' :

Depressed = Deep Rest. "Of course", I thought. Deep rest. After a period of psychic stress - grief, trauma, intensity of any kind, good or bad - our biology requires a period of rest to integrate the event(s) and re-stabilize at a new level of growth; find renewed homeostasis. Perhaps if we can recognize this re-integration need as a normal transformational stage versus a pathology that must be corrected, we could lose the fear/anxiety about it and find appropriate self-care in some form that suits us. We may even learn to *allow* ourselves to enjoy such due rest, although admittedly, that may be a stretch at first for some of us conditioned otherwise. The more we allow ourselves such rest as our system needs at such times, the more we can thoroughly learn from these experiences and the more quickly we can through them and move on.

This view differs significantly from our cultural hypnosis of regarding such states as pathologically wrong or bad. Thus, it may reduce the concomitant fear and anxiety in such states. Sadness, for example, may not be one's favorite emotional state. However, if we remove the cultural misbeliefs or stigma associated with it, it's not necessarily painful. We can learn to listen to it, rest with it, gain the message or learning it's laden with and move on that much healthier and stronger.

In the former condition, we had sadness + fear of having the sadness, which fosters suffering. In the more enlightened approach, without the compulsory fear, we have something quite different.

In **_Iron John_**, (Da Capo Press, 1990), Robert Bly repeatedly suggests that grief serves us. It brings us down to earth and back to our deeper selves so that we may effectively heal old wounds that we perhaps have tried to avoid. In returning to these wounds and hurts, we may heal and become whole.

Tears of sadness and tears of joy come from the same well.

The more we continue to block or deny a feeling, the more we block its antithesis. The more we block sadness, the more we limit our ability to allow deep joy in our experience whenever it may want to be felt. Sadness and joy are feelings germane to the heart center or heart chakra. To block those feelings is to block our vital conduit to our divinity through the heart. Not advisable.

One of my greatest spiritual teachers said, *"When sadness knocks at the door, by all means, **by all means**, let yourself feel it! ... Just don't take it too seriously."* (Or as I like to say, don't take it too 'severiously'.)

Depth is a wonderful quality in humans. What a flat existence it would be without. Denial of feelings creates flatness of being. Honoring our feelings fosters depth, interest, increased potential for intimacy, creativity and much more. And when it's time to celebrate, our joy will be deeper and more real.

7. THE TECHNOLOGY OF FORGIVENESS ™

Forgiveness: What is it really, what is it *not*, and how do we do it?

Over the years, I noticed many spiritual teachings emphasizing the importance of forgiveness in our healing and spiritual development. In A Course in Miracles, a book addressing many essential spiritual matters, forgiveness is mentioned over 200 times. In my experience, if there is one thing that stands out as a most powerful tool in healing and awakening, particularly at this time of human and planetary transformation, it is forgiveness of self and others.

Blockages

To lead into the subject, I'd like to first discuss blockages. Blockages within us restrict the natural flow of love in any of its forms—including love itself, healing, clarity, abundance, communion with one's Higher Power, and others—from being a part of our daily existence.

The first blockage is **fear**, which includes anger, guilt, and shame. It is important to feel, express, release, and learn from any feeling in order to remove the blockage. It is natural for living beings to have fear from time to time, and it is counterproductive to judge ourselves for it.

Denial is the second blockage. We deny only what we fear. Unfortunately, the act of denial creates the opposite of what we wish for. Instead of removing something from one's reality, the object of denial (the feeling, the secret, or the fear) is intensified to the extent that it consumes most, if not all, of our attention because we're busy making certain that door stays shut.

An Acid test to illustrate this: For the next 5 seconds, do not think about blue giraffes.

OK - What just happened? Did you think about blue giraffes? Or did you 'jump track' and force yourself to think about something else, perhaps orange turtles?

Either way, you required yourself to *not* think about blue giraffes. Part of your consciousness busy remembering to 'keep that door shut' and not think about blue giraffes. As with any form of denial, part of your consciousness is working hard to think about something else. This is poor psychic economy. This may occur at a conscious or unconscious level. It is essential to identify and relinquish the denial, including processing the underlying fear. *Acceptance* of WHAT IS allows us to process and move through the issue, whereas denial will only fester, intensify, and likely find expression that is, in some way, harmful to self and others.

The third blockage is **judgment**. As with denial, we only judge what we fear and haven't come to terms with. In the act of judging, we project thoughts from the past onto whomever or whatever we're observing, to an extent that prevents clear perception. This blockage detracts greatly from our ability to effectively proceed on our paths. It is unprocessed fear that fuels such an impasse, and it is that fear which we must embrace and process, as well as being willing to simply drop our judgments as much as humanly possible. Doing this will allow us passage *through* the blockage.

We gain from forgiving ourselves or otherwise come to terms with a quality or behavior within ourselves that we might project upon another person. Then, as we observe that person displaying such behavior, there will be little or no emotional charge remaining. This will tell us that we are current in self-forgiveness regarding the issue in question.

Ingratitude is the fourth blockage. As we observed in the 'Blue Giraffe' exercise, denial focuses most of our attention on the object of denial to the extent that our efforts toward managing that object becomes what our life is about. We attract, or magnetize into our experience, that which we fear and want to deny in such a scenario. Gratitude can similarly direct our beam of attention toward that which we're willing to feel grateful for. In redirecting our attention, we attract into our experience more of what we may feel grateful for. We have our part in what we attract. Feeling gratitude opens our heart center and allows a healthy flow of love in its many forms to move into our experience. We do not force ourselves to feel gratitude in the midst of pain that we may be dealing with—that would be denial. I'd suggest that we honor and process *all* feeling states sufficiently and become willing to notice and feel what we can be grateful for in our lives. There's always something to be grateful for, if we're willing to pause and observe.

Gratitude and forgiveness are literally very close in their measurable vibratory rate. Both states have the effect of opening that most vital conduit to Spirit or our Higher Power, the heart center, through which we can connect with the highest and deepest wisdom that we all are wired for.

The last blockage in this discussion is **non-forgiveness of self and/or others.** If we imagine all of these blockages as logs in our stream of love in all of its forms, then lack of forgiveness would be the biggest log blocking our stream. Let's explore forgiveness in greater depth.

What forgiveness is and isn't

By definition, forgiveness is simply the willingness or choice to release or let go of a grievance, grudge, or resentment. That's all. Simple.

As important as it is to know what forgiveness means, it's equally important to know what it does *not* mean there has been much confusion about this in our culture.

First, forgiveness does not mean that you condone a behavior that's unacceptable to you. Second, it does not mean that you must become a victim of someone's hurtful behavior. It serves no one to let that part of creation that you are become victimized. Third, forgiveness does not require that you forget something hurtful that may have happened. Requiring oneself to forget would not be release, but denial. The phrase "forgive and forget" has its place, yet forgiveness does not require forgetting. An acid test to be certain that we are current in our forgiveness is that when we think of the issue in question, there is little or no emotional charge left. **If there is still an emotional charge, we know that feelings remain that need honoring and processing.**

Often we speak of forgiveness in terms of ability: "I was/was not able to forgive him." In misusing the words *able* or *ability* here, we dupe ourselves into believing that forgiveness rests upon some ability that we do or do not possess. In fact, forgiveness has nothing to do with ability. If you're able to understand these words, you're able to forgive.

Forgiveness has everything to do with willingness and choice.

Before we find our willingness to forgive, there are two areas to examine. First, are we current in honoring and processing the *feelings* associated with the event? There are no "negative" feelings, and all true feelings are worth processing and deriving gifts of awareness from.

Second, are there *reasons* that we've accepted to withhold forgiveness? What fear-based reasons have we bought into through family and society that we use to justify the withholding of forgiveness? Let's take a look at a few of the more typical reasons.

1. Protection: "If I don't forgive her, I'll be protected from being hurt by her again." Or, "If I don't forgive myself, then I'll be certain I won't do that again."

2. Punishment: "If I don't forgive him, that will pay him back, or at least he'll have to feel what I felt and don't want to feel again."

3. Self-righteousness/Pride: "If I don't forgive them, I'll feel better than they are, and I won't need to take a look at my part in what occurred between us."

4. Distance a Relationship: "If I don't forgive him, that will create a safe distance between us, and I won't have to deal with him." (This is similar to protection.)

5. Keep a Relationship: "If I don't forgive her, and if I feel that non-forgiveness is the only thread to hang on to an otherwise defunct relationship, then I can hold on to at least some part of a relationship that I'm afraid to let go of."

Here is the pivotal point in understanding the technology of forgiveness: Keeping in mind the blockages that we discussed earlier, who suffers *most* when one chooses to withhold forgiveness? Whose stream of love is blocked most in non-forgiveness? Is there any question? Is it not clear that the one who withholds forgiveness is the one who would suffer the most? - The one whose stream of love is blocked the most? Others may suffer too, in not having the openness of relationship with you that they may otherwise enjoy. But who suffers the most? Clearly, it's the non-forgiver.

With this pivotal understanding, what happens to these old, erroneous "reasons" to not forgive?

1. Protection: If anything, you need protection from yourself in any choice to withhold forgiveness because you'd be suffering more than anyone else from that choice.

2. Punishment: Who is being punished the most? Given the theme of Primal Unity wherein all life is intimately connected or is One, if you were to generate hurtful thoughts or actions toward anyone/any living thing or part of creation, whom would you be hurting? Call it God, All That Is, yourself, all of life, . . . there is

50

little difference.

3. Self-righteousness / Pride: This is a curious one. You've traveled this far in your spiritual journey of embodiment in this planetary schoolhouse of Earth, so why assume the posture of self-righteousness, which, in effect, pushes your lessons away from you? That would be a poor personal economy, indeed.

4. Distance a Relationship: By forgiving, we can clear our stream and we can set a clear boundary (not to be confused with 'threat') with another in order to take care of ourselves. We needn't harm ourselves any further with non-forgiveness.

5. Keep a Relationship: If this is all that's left of a relationship, why not 'let go and let God' as it's often said, and let another relationship occur in time? Hanging on, white-knuckled, out of fear will surely choke and kill anything that's left of a relationship, as well as feeding the fearful illusions of scarcity or lack. If we let go, we can see if there's something to salvage from that relationship or clear our hearts to make room for a more appropriate one.

It is now clear that it makes poor sense to withhold forgiveness. When we don't forgive another, we're giving them free rent in our heads - a very self-defeating posture - and we would remain stuck.

"There are two kinds of people in the world: those who have what they want in life and those who have *reasons* for not having what they want. Which type of person do you wish to be?" - Werner Erhard, 1977

Consider the following questions when thinking of the people you haven't forgiven:

1. Is it possible that they were in fear when they did or said what they did?

2. Is it possible that there was poor, or even a lack of, communication between you?

3. Is it possible that those individuals were doing the best they

51

knew how to do at the time, given where they came from?

4. Is it possible that you had expectations beyond their capability at that time?

5. What did you learn about yourself in having had contact with those individuals? Is it valuable to you now?

6. If the behavior of others was particularly hurtful, ask yourself: Where did they learn such behavior? What might have happened in their development which led them to cut off their hearts so?

7. What has it cost you to withhold forgiveness? What is the price you've been paying *over time*?

8. Are you *willing* to forgive now?

If you do not feel ready to forgive at this point, do not judge yourself. Rather, let such a process show you *exactly* where your blockage may be, i.e., what feelings need processing or what reasons need review.

If you do feel willing to forgive, a simple visualizing process will assist you in envisioning the person that you wish to forgive, as they look at you calmly, as you remember them, feeling their presence. You may also forgive yourself in this way, visualizing yourself at the age pertaining to the event that you wish to forgive.

Consider the above questions carefully, one-by-one. Breathing deeply and slowly, simply breathe it out and release the grievance, grudge, or resentment, for it is history. Later, simply notice what might feel different in the area of your heart.

As you forgive and thus remove a major blockage in the channel of love that you are, it would be realistic to expect some change in your life. For three days following your forgiveness of self or another, gently be aware of anything that feels as though movement or a shift is occurring and allow yourself to feel gratitude for your willingness to forgive, let go, release, and move on.

The late Lisa de Longchamps, who founded the Wingsong School in Oakland, California, during the 1970s, has brilliantly shared many such understandings that clarify forgiveness and its importance. For example, she suggests that forgiveness is of a vibration that transmutes karma, or the need to repeat certain lessons along life's path.

She also taught that a key factor in any kind of healing—physical or emotional—is the forgiveness of self and/or others, pointing out that non-forgiveness is supported by the misconception of making another person your Source. You may not receive what you think you want from someone, yet that does not mean that the universe is not yearning to support you through other means. Lisa would often refer to the behavior of bees: If a bee flies to a field of flowers, lights upon one flower and quickly learns that its nectar has been consumed by another bee, what does the bee do? Does it stay and kick that flower? No. It simply lights upon another flower. There are times when we have much to learn from bees.

Lisa would stress the importance of accepting your own forgiveness, and that the refusal to accept it and the insistence of punishing yourself with guilt is a form of arrogance that will exact a great price from you and, therefore, those in your life. Guilt, as with any feeling, offers a valuable lesson when honored. It shows us where our values are; what is important to our core being. Then, we are clearly informed as to how to best trim our sails and behave differently in order to preserve our true values. Dwelling in guilt beyond its lesson is of no value.

Self-forgiveness can be practiced every day without being overdone. It is said that God forgives us totally. Another viewpoint is that the Creator doesn't need to forgive us because He/She doesn't condemn us.

Studies of the near-death experience (NDE) from ancient and modern sources alike show a very high correlation throughout the data. During the stage following rapid movement through a long data. During the stage following rapid movement through a long tunnel toward the light, near-death experiencers often report a scene in which, typically, one experiences a gathering of many of the important players in one's lifetime. At such a gathering the experiencer may walk up to one who played the role of their most formidable antagonist, perpetrator, or enemy. The NDE'r might look at this person in the eye and say, "Thank you for volunteering to play your role so well. You really helped me focus on what I so much wanted to learn in this lifetime. Thank you!"

Similarly, Lao-Tzu, founder of Taoism, said, "No one is your friend. No one is your enemy. Everyone is your teacher."

We are all teachers and students, serving each other in many ways in this planetary schoolhouse.

Phillip Mitchell's CD, *THE TECHNOLOGY OF FORGIVENESS,* is available at the Sierra Tucson Bookstore, 800-624-9001. It includes guided visualization for forgiveness and 2 other topics.

8. The Heart of Livelihood

Many of us are more aware of work activities that are no longer compatible with our evolving nature, versus alternate activities that may inspire us. Some of us have experienced fatigue or burnout in our employment, which indicates that our activity is no longer suitable. Sometimes we've noticed other activities or people engaged in something that piques our interest, only to quiet ourselves with thoughts of "shoulds" that we've bought into and beliefs like "Maybe she can do that, but it would be too impractical for me to make a living at it."

How sad that we've learned to discredit the importance of doing what's fun. In examining more closely the anatomy of fun, one finds that it is connected with, and enlivening to, our heart center, that vital conduit to our higher and deeper knowing. It is associated with that which offers us a greater aliveness, pleasure and joy that, as Tiellard de Chardin has suggested, is the surest sign of the presence of the Creator.

Joseph Campbell often spoke of the importance of "following your bliss. When we commit to that, doors of opportunity open for us that we could not have accounted for before making that commitment." Campbell, one of the finest scholars of world mythology, also suggested that underneath the innumerable tales and myths from all cultures, there is only one story: The central figure surmounts hardships, slays dragons and rebuffs that particular society's *shoulds* in favor of following the dictates of the heart, the deeper knowing. This central character, the hero/heroine, emerges victorious, realizing his/her dream in doing so.

Many feel that life is worth living only when we identify and follow our own hero's journey.

Those doubting the practicality of following the heart will do well to consider that only when the heart is involved in one's daily activity can one realize the fullest and most enduring success.

In spiritual perspective, when we follow our heart, and our essence expresses through the heart, we allow that aspect of the Creator to express through us, as us, as only we can express it. Our energy, knowing and ability expands. Joyfulness and gratitude replace negativity and doubt. What a loss to ourselves and the world it would be not to express and share our unique contribution to life.

Those who respond with, "Sure, I'd love to switch gears and follow my heart more, but that would be too scary," let me ask which is scarier: living another several years of your precious gift of life in fear and stuckness, or taking some healthy risks now in finding and realizing your heart path?

I'd like to offer some suggestions and hints that will help to actualize your path of the heart.

1. Follow Your Excitement

First, as Bashar suggests, *excitement.* Pay attention to what excites you most, in small ways as well as in big ones. Commit to following that excitement and let the universe lead you to more of it.

If the most exciting thing that you can imagine doing is not available to you in that moment, large or small, then act on the next most exciting thing and trust that it will lead further into your excitement. Excitement is a reliable indicator of doing what you came here to do; of being on purpose. Acting on your excitement will also raise your vibration, making it easier to attract more of what you would prefer in life.

As Lisa deLongchamps suggested, find out what you enjoy doing so much that you'd pay to do it. Make that your livelihood and let people pay you to do it. Or ask yourself, "If my finances were of no concern, how would I most enjoy spending my time?"

Review *shoulds* and *oughts* that you've bought into from family and society. Let the clutter of those that no longer fit you fall away. (And be cautious of *shoulding* on your children and others.)

Honor the importance of play. Create healthy amounts of playtime in your schedule and play with following your heart.

Give up rigid beliefs and pictures of what your livelihood should look like. Understand that one's divine expression may *take many turns in its course* and need not conform to a lifelong career model.

Practice relaxing your cognitive functioning whenever possible in support of allowing other valuable ways of knowing and perceiving to emerge. Meditation, deep and slow breathing practices, honoring feeling states, and physical and creative activity that are fun will support you this way.

Overconcern with money is a common smokescreen. Relax the notion that you must have a certain amount of money to do what's in your heart to do. If it's truly appropriate for you to do, let people know of your interest, find a way to begin and get involved in that activity. Money will follow as a natural by-product of following your Divine Plan.

Don't be discouraged by initial obstacles or doubters. It seems that the universe places them in our path to test our resolve. It is as though you are being asked, "Are you sure this is what you want?" to test your resolve. This can have the effect of helping you sharpen your focus and garner the requisite energy and resources to begin. It would almost be unfortunate, or at least less interesting, if such forces were not present. Consider welcoming and appreciating such forces in this broader perspective.

Consider how your products or services will benefit others and the planet. Many prominent teachers agree that service to life is the most fulfilling focus of livelihood. In the words of Bengali poet, Rabindranath Tagore:

I slept and dreamt that life was joy,

I woke and saw that life was service,

I acted — and behold, service was joy.

"Work is love made visible. If you cannot work with love, but only with distaste, it is better to leave your work and sit at the gate of the temple and take alms of those who work with joy. For if you bake bread with indifference, you bake a bitter bread that feeds but half our hunger." - Kahlil Gibran

9. *REALAXING*

Stress may be one of the effects of the accelerated change in our midst. The challenge of maintaining equanimity or at least a semblance of peace is intensifying. It is all too clear that in order to be an instrument of peace, we must know how to access and nurture it within.

A few keys that can be particularly effective for sane navigation as we approach the Great Shift:

1. Do you breathe? Much attention from various disciplines has been given to the importance of breath, and for good reason. The Latin derivation of our word "spirit" (*spiritus*) means breath, wind, energy, as do *ruach, prana, pneuma, chi* and *ki* in other languages. This infinite ocean of life that we participate in is spirit. To breathe fully is to awaken, inform, enliven, spiritualize that aspect of spirit which manifests as our being.

Full breathing is the essence of yoga, meditation, healing, visualization, emotional release, expanded awareness and so on. Yet how often are we aware of its importance? Typically, in any state of fear we slow or stop our breathing.

In Yoga and other practices, there are innumerable breathing techniques, each inducing a certain state of consciousness or being. The type of breathing that I'd like to encourage here is generic and simple: deep, slow, even breath - deep, down to your heels; slow, with matched inhalation and exhalation, and a slight pause in between, like a big circle of breath that's breathing you. The exhalation need not be forced or blown out, as during aerobic exercise. Rather, let the breath "fall" out naturally, easily, with little *do-ing*.

Practicing such breathing is totally safe and cannot be overdone. The breather will soon notice relaxation occurring and feel a sense of peace, without using any outside substance or elaborate technique.

It is so simple, in fact, that you can do it in the midst of chaos to center yourself, and no one is likely to notice. When we reach the peaceful wakefulness that true breathing offers, we can best access healing, clarity, peace, knowing and unconditional love for self and others, which is so necessary in this evolutionary moment.

2. **Deepened acceptance of our universal education model.** Certain core themes are shared by many spiritual teachings, regardless of dimension, time or origin. One such example is the idea that our current home planet serves as the schoolhouse where we chose to learn. Ultimately, all there is to learn is that we are an expression of love, the 'glue' of the universe, the essence of the Creator. To learn what love is, we have chosen to learn what it is not. Hence, the infinite permutations of our collective physical experience.

If one enters school, it is wise to select a curriculum, is it not? Our very issues in life are our curricula. Would you judge another for selecting a curriculum of interest at a local university? Probably not. Why judge yourselves for having your own curriculum?

When we are willing to accept the idea that regardless of current memory, we chose, at some level of our being, every stitch of our physical experience, dropping the senseless, fear-based judgment that may surface, we may relax into knowing that all is well despite appearances If we are willing to accept that all we experience is necessarily perfect in its unfolding, it's easier to learn from these experiences and make appropriate responses. There's nothing left to fight, judge or worry about.

Here again, as we use the tool of deep, slow breathing, it's easier to slow down so we can catch up with ourselves and remember such understandings.

Dr. Carl Jung often stated that whatever the situation or dilemma we find ourselves in, implicit in it is our ability to deal with it. Otherwise it wouldn't be there. Remember this point, too, as you breathe and slow down sufficiently to see with greater clarity.

3. **A gift of retrospect.** Have you ever noticed when you pause and reflect upon the myriad events, activities and pursuits of love and livelihood, that regardless of the apparent disparities, there is a thread of continuity that links them? And that somehow all of this collected experience has prepared you for the present moment as well as your next step?

Why not hold this awareness sufficiently to notice that your present moment, whatever the appearance, is necessarily a perfect opportunity to prepare for whatever is next on your path. Are you willing to appreciate the present as you might appreciate certain views of your past? There are no mistakes. All that transpires is a gift of learning and a step toward what's next. How's that for inner peacemaking, not to mention joy-making?

4. **Choose trust.** Bashar sums this up nicely.* He states that when the subject of trust comes up in a group, he is often met with a collective groan, "Everyone knows that it's hard to trust *all* the time!" He usually responds with humor, stating that we have never stopped trusting in something for one moment of our lives. The question is, do we choose to trust in a negative reality according to past (illusory) beliefs, or are we willing to trust in a reality we prefer?

We do have that option to choose, including the choice to drop all worry, a very destructive thing. What we trust or believe in, good or bad, is what we will out-picture and experience. The universe is neutral in this process and will faithfully reflect whatever program we select.

This area has been a challenge on my path at times, yet I am grateful to be learning the subtle art of redirecting my trust more and more in a direction of preference.

5. **The economics of honesty and openness**. Have you noticed how much work it takes to keep a secret or to remember the details of a falsehood in the event it might be probed? Much precious life energy is wasted here, not to mention the stress such behavior incurs. If we're dishonest with anyone, we're ultimately dishonest with ourselves and thus thwart our own evolution.

Thomas Merton once said, "If there were to be but one religious path, let it be that of honesty." Life is much simpler and cleaner when we walk that way. At the same time, being human, let us forgive ourselves for being less than 100% honest all the time.

6. **"Simplify, simplify, simplify."** - Henry D. Thoreau. Whatever you do, whatever project you undertake, whatever you consider purchasing, ask yourself, "How can this be made simpler, more fun?" (from Lisa deLongchamps). Spirituality is simplicity itself. Complexity is the adversary that can take us away from our unfettered spiritual center.

When St. Francis of Assisi beckoned his followers to "do little," he didn't mean "do nothing." He meant to avoid becoming so busy that you've left yourself no time to remember who you are (a part of the Creator) and why you're here — to teach and share love. Of course, sometimes doing nothing, being vs. doing, can be the most productive and meaningful thing to "do." Next time you say that you're too busy to do something you'd enjoy doing, ask yourself, "Who arranges and prioritizes my schedule, anyway?"

7. Find an animal companion. When did you last spend time with a pet or other nonhuman being of this planet? They have so much to share with us and teach us, do they not? They come to our realm, often at great sacrifice, to demonstrate the most important thing (yes, unconditional love). They offer their entire being to us so we can practice loving, and they help us fine-tune our knowing about what love is. They also offer, by their modeling, a host of other lessons; the importance of playfulness, what's important in life and what's not, trusting your instincts, how to relax and much more. Notice how they relax, stretch, play, nap, groom - and know exactly when to perform these functions.

Innumerable studies show that people who have pets tend to live longer, happier lives. Your local animal shelter is probably teeming with orphaned animals who would love nothing more than to play, in love, with you.

(Incidentally, Bashar has stated that cats in particular function in more than one dimension simultaneously and thus model that ability to us. This is quite significant, given that the nature of the soon-to-come Great Shift will require of us such abilities.)

8. Walk in nature, even if all that's available to you is a city park. Do anything to support your connection to our Earth home and feel her pulse. Walk barefoot when possible. Experience the sights, scents, sounds, love and information She continually imparts.

One could go on indefinitely with good ideas for reducing stress and finding peace. I chose to focus on the above ideas because they are sometimes overlooked, and too exhaustive a list might defeat the purpose of slowing down and simplifying. If one were to truly integrate a handful of ideas such as these, a profound change for the better would result.

Breathe. . .

*Bashar through Daryl Anka; various audiotapes, CD's, DVD's

available at: www.Bashar.org

**Maggie Pym, a friend in British Columbia, states, "Cats are wondrous beings — they will jump-start the most closed-up heart chakra."

10. Toning for Healing and Awakening

Toning, in a broad sense, is the channeling and use of voice or sound for transformation. The transformation might include healing, manifesting, spiritual initiation and awakening, interdimensional communication and more. It is an ancient art that was used in Atlantis, Syriad (now Egypt), Tibet, India, various aboriginal, shamanistic cultures and extra-dimensionally. It has been predicted that light and sound would be the prime tools of healing and awakening in the Golden Age, and their renewed popularity is already evident.

Everything in our manifest universe is at a certain state of vibration. To direct sound/vibration toward any object or being is to change it.* The nature of the change will be in accordance with the conscious intention of the being or beings generating or channeling the tones.

Toning usually refers to, but is not limited to, the human voice. Alternate modalities include instruments such as the didgeridoo, cetacean (whale and dolphin) communication, communication of elephants and other large mammals over distances of many miles and smaller animals such as bats and various insects, etc.

Many of us have heard the powerfully transformative toning in the chants of the Tibetan Gyöto monks and know that in hearing and feeling such sounds, we are transformed in some way. The work of David Hykes' Harmonic Choir is equally powerful in its own right. It is also intriguing to listen to the creative adaptation of toning in the recordings and performances of Toby Twining's ensemble.

Since the demise of the Soviet Union as we knew it, Westerners have been able to hear the incredible sounds of the Tuvan throat singers of Mongolia. They draw from a rich shamanic heritage.

Recordings of the Tuvan group *Huun-Huur-Tu* are now available in Western countries.

Also remarkable is the a cappella singing of the Bulgarian Women's Choir. Their mixture of Slavic, proto-Bulgarian and Thracian musical elements with intricate points of dissonance is a transformation in itself to experience. Some listeners claim they sense strains of Atlantean and Sirian influence in some of their songs. Their recordings are also widely available.

The vibrations of light (particularly through sacred geometry) and sound are encoded with literal in-form-action that induces cellular awakening in the channel and the receiver. Much of the channeled toning coming through toners carries the light/knowledge of fifth-dimensional levels and beyond that cannot be comprehended cognitively, yet we are impacted by it on a cellular or soul level.

Chants, songs, melodies or simply pleasurable sounds can have a healing effect too. When a tone becomes multiphonic (carrying two or more notes simultaneously), its power to permeate matter, including bodies, is greatly increased. Much of the chanting of Tibetan monks is multiphonic; the carrier note is most audible, complemented by overtones. Often there are more than two simultaneous notes, but many humans cannot yet distinguish them all.

Spiritual initiation rites utilize toning to punctuate and to accelerate the attainment of higher levels of consciousness. Such toning and chanting would also take the form of words of the ancient sacred languages such as Aramaic, Hebrew and Sanskrit. Precise pronunciation of these words by the priests and masters was essential because correct pronunciation constitutes specific sequences or combinations of vibrations that are necessary to activate soul memory and the awakening of the initiate.

Much can be learned about toning in the audio tapes and books of Don Campbell and Jonathan Goldman. Campbell emphasizes the value of making natural sounds expressive of feeling as an introduction to toning. Goldman focuses more on learning to produce overtones.

One simple approach in producing a vocal overtone is to experiment with the subtle vowel sound between *eee* and *ooo*. A private contained space (perhaps inside your car while driving) or going outside in nature can be fine places to practice. Be patient. When you begin to hear the overtone, play with it, changing the shape of your mouth, position of your tongue, dilation of your throat and nasal cavity, until you are capable of producing the overtone at will. At this point you can be more creative and see what amazing sounds you can allow to come through.

My guidance discouraged a formal study of toning. Rather, I was encouraged to let spirit prompt and guide me in remembering and opening to channel tones. I was encouraged to practice it outside in nature whenever I would feel the impulse, and to move my hands to assist supporting the tones in coming through. Over the years this approach has been delightful and successful. Some readers may be inspired to engage in a formal training in toning.

When toning for emotional or physical healing with a human or othe animal, I align with Jesus/Yeshua/Sananda, as best I can, to ensure that whatever comes through will provide the greatest good for all involved. This has to do with clear, heart-centered intention. Use any method comfortable to you in accessing your heart-knowing.

Tones can be directed into any part of the body or may affect all of one's being to implement healing or awakening. Do not be concerned with the sounds being pleasant to your taste. The effectiveness and appropriateness of a tone has little to do with this.

With practice, one can learn to sense what kinds of tones are most appropriate for various applications, as well as what intensity and duration is most fitting. After toning, it is important that the toner and receiver remain silent for a minute or two to allow the transformative effect its due course. Any words too soon may cancel the effectiveness of the toning.

*Dr. Hans Jenny, a Swiss scientist, pioneered the study of *Cymatics*, which shows how sound organizes in basic structures of sacred geometry in sand and other mediums.

Some Additional References:

1. For those interested in the shamanic uses of toning, refer to the work of Joan Halifax, Ph.D.

2. The book Starseed: The Third Millennium by Ken Carey remains one of the most beautifully written, spiritually oriented books I've ever read. Chapter 19, "Songs of Distinction," offers wonderful insight into toning.

3. In Bringers of the Dawn by Barbara Marciniak, Chapter 18, "Symphonies of Consciousness," there are more interesting insights into ancient uses of toning.

"... you will remember how to sing the songs that only awakened humans can sing, songs that will bring metals up from the ground, songs that will attract elements, minerals, materials, from across great distances, through the power of their true names." - from Starseed: The Third Millenium, Ken Carey, Harper Collins, 1991, Ch. 19.

11. TAKE ME BY THE HAND: A LOOK AT NEAR-DEATH EXPERIENCE AND ITS RELEVANCE TO RECOVERY AND SPIRITUAL AWAKENING

"No one is your friend. No one is your enemy. Everyone is your teacher."

- Lao Tzu

The study of near-death experience (NDE) in recent decades has proliferated. This focus has much to do with, and has many parallels with ancient and contemporary spiritual teachings as well as with recovery and healing. There is much correlation between the ancient writings - Egyptian, Mayan, Hindu, Qabalistic, Hopi and more - with modern studies of NDE. These understandings are drawn from a variety of teachings on the subject and focus on some of their commonalities.

One of the first understandings that students of NDE and spirituality find is, contrary to our common Western cultural view, no one 'dies' as we have thought. Of course, we shed the physical body when it's no longer functional or useful, or if it's irreparably damaged. However one's essence, whether we refer to it as Spirit, Soul, Prana, Sheckinah, etc., continues its existence. Humans and all lifeforms are seen as aspects of the Creator / God, and no part of the Creator can cease to exist. We are all part of the eternal. We have always existed and always will.

A more appropriate word for death may be *transition.* Of course, in this physical dimension, when we have the experience of losing someone close to us through what we have called 'death', that is a loss which deserves a proper grieving process. Such a process requires time, sometimes ritual and support in grieving the loss with free expression of feelings. As we are first spiritual beings and secondly physical beings, we benefit from honoring the full physical life experience. (This is referred to as *lebenvelt* or 'lived-world experience' for the phenomenologists).

The physical realm is the densest of the many dimensions of existence. If likened to a boat race, we must round the furthest (densest) buoy; otherwise we are disqualified from the event. We benefit and learn from embracing grief and all emotion as part and parcel of the physical journey. Our incarnation is largely for the purpose of experiencing and learning from all that we encounter in life. Another point of view is that our physical life is our *most* lucid dream.

- Bashar

There is a story of a great spiritual teacher who taught his disciples that all of physical existence was no more than an illusion and serves as metaphoric *allusion* to greater spiritual truths. One day his son died suddenly and he grieved and sobbed heavily for some time. His students were perplexed by this and one asked, "Master - you tell us that this realm is all illusion, yet you grieve so much for your son! How can this be?" The Master responded saying, "Because this is the most difficult illusion of all."

It seems that nearly all of life's lessons entail some form or some level of letting go. Letting go of our physical bodies and our physical existence may be the ultimate *letting go* that we experience here. Interestingly, according to many teachers, what we have referred to as 'death' can be a much easier process than what we refer to as 'birth'.

When a person becomes cognizant of the imminence of their transition from the physical, certain signs are common. There is often less interest in 'chit-chat' and greater interest in more meaningful discourse, especially with those they feel closest to. I suspect this is why many in the helping professions are drawn to working with the dying and to hospice work. People tend to be very real at such times. Warm, gentle touch becomes increasingly important, including the holding of hands.

Often a realization of what's truly important in life arises as one nears their transition. Worldly achievement, acquisitions, wealth, social status, knowledge or fame have lost importance. Not that such *glamours* were 'bad'. All 'props' that we choose in life are neutral. Their purpose is to serve us in the physical journey so that we can most effectively extract the lessons we desired to experience within a specific lifetime.

What usually holds greatest importance as one nears transition is *how much and how well have we learned to share love* in this lifetime. Little else seems to matter. This is very instructive to remember as we navigate the waters of physical life.

STAGES OF TRANSITION

There is usually a sequence of experiences reported both in the ancient teachings as well as modern NDE studies. Of course there can be many variations of the following, yet these stages will frequently occur.

The **Life Review Stage** consists of seeing, experiencing and feeling your impact on others throughout your lifetime, yet somehow, in an instant. No one outside yourself judges you. You may judge yourself or re-evaluate and learn from your thoughts, words and actions.

Many ND Experiencers report the awareness of very rapidly moving through a **long, spiral tunnel** next. For those that have seen the movie 'Contact', the main character's interdimensional travel sequence is often referred to as quite realistic and similar to this experience for many.

At the end of the Tunnel stage, there is a **Reconvening**. Here, in an illumined area, one sees all the important players of their lifetime - embodied, usually in their prime-of-life bodies or as the transitioner remembers them. These souls will usually act as caring guides for the newly transitioned soul in exploring new/old realms.

At some point afterward, they enter the **pure light**. This is where ND Experiencers often report gloriously beautiful experiences of color, music, grace, peace, clear vision and more. One wonderful account of this is the 1982 NDE of artist Mellen-Thomas Benedict whose personal account is of extraordinary beauty and joy. Frequently, the experiencer returns to this realm with vivid recollection of their experience, a deep sense of peace, clarity of their purpose and a good deal of love and wisdom to share. We have much to learn from those who have experienced 'the beyond' as well as such experiences that we may have in the physical.

There are many implications of this body of information as they apply to recovery, healing and spiritual growth. Meanwhile, if you are present and identified with a body while reading this, your work and learning here is not done. May you enjoy the remainder of your tour of this realm.

http://www.near-death.com/geometry.html

12. Predictions

During a workshop of Deepak Chopra, he shared that upon asking his young son what he'd like in the upcoming year, the boy replied, *"I want even more uncertainty than I experienced this year so that I can feel more joy."*

As I chuckled, I realized the wonderful value of such a view. I also reflected on ways in which I've been over-reliant on predictions in an attempt to control my future. In doing so I haven't allowed myself to live fully in the present, which holds all the information I need for choosing my next step. Or to be truly present in my life. I missed the joy and aliveness that the present offers in my futile attempt to control a future that is not real.

Thought and behavior that attempt to control are a result of fears that haven't been honored, felt, expressed and released. It's difficult to let the many forms of joy and love flow when undue attention is given to fear, by either denying it or attempting to control it.

As many people progress in their spiritual development, it becomes increasingly clear that although a spiritual teacher/guide, guru or channel may be of great value on one's path, it is important not to give too much power away at the expense of failing to listen to the guidance of one's own heart. In the area of healing and medicine I've often seen people either heal or become more ill by virtue of the power they've given or not given to the healing practitioner. Similarly, the power given to predictions has much to do with the likelihood of their manifesting.

I do not wish to cast a blanket negative judgment or shadow upon all types of prediction, nor would I upon any field of activity. There are appropriate times to work with predictions. Rather, I want to be more aware of the misuses and pitfalls of some predictive activity and share this awareness.

One area of proliferating predictions is Earth changes. There has been a general agreement that this decade would be one of dramatic Earth changes, yet there are ways to view this other than from a literal, third-dimensional perspective.

For example, in The Nature of Personal Reality by Jane Roberts (Bantam Books, 1978), Seth explained that if two friends are sitting on a couch, one may experience an earthquake (metaphorically, a shaking-up of one's reality) if he/she needs that experience at that moment, whereas the other person on the couch may not experience it. This idea alludes to the multidimensionality of the universe and the multiple and parallel universes that we each create. In this light, universal prediction is not possible.

Sometimes a prediction will motivate us. It may or may not materialize, but in hearing it, we change

and the prediction has thus served its purpose.

Another idea that could skew the accuracy or relevance of prediction is that, because of our connectedness or oneness with the Earth, the inner work we do with ourselves (clearing and harmonizing our issues and lessons) directly impacts the Earth and all life. This effect is usually one of healing, which reduces the need for the Earth to react or mirror events for us in a violent manner to attract our attention.

"Learn to listen to the whispers... so you won't have to hear the screams." - Lazaris

In Bashar: Blueprint for Change by Darryl Anka (New Solutions, 1990), he stated that a prediction is valid only in the moment it's made. In the next moment, everything is changed and the prediction no longer applies. He also suggests that sometimes a prediction will motivate us to move in a certain direction. The prediction may or may not materialize, but in hearing it, we change as necessary, and the prediction has thus served its purpose.

Many of us on spiritual paths consider planning for the future, and this is not a bad thing. It's appropriate to steer our ship in a desired direction. Yet given the accelerated change that we and our planet are experiencing, we increasingly sense the futility of planning, or at least have less attachment to a specific outcome.

As with any prophecy or form of divination, there may be great value in seeing which way the winds are blowing in order to best trim our sails.

However, when you are honoring the knowing within your own heart, let that knowing take share validity with any information you expose yourself to from 'outside' of yourself.

"Tell me what you are for, and I will show you what is going to expand in a positive way. Tell me what you are against, and I will show you what is going to expand in a destructive way."

- Dr. Wayne Dyer

About the Author

Phillip S. Mitchell is a highly experienced Psychotherapist practicing at a major mental health and addiction rehab facility in the desert mountains outside of Tucson, Arizona. He draws from a rich blend of psychological and spiritual orientations including Gestalt, Jungian, Family Systems and Transpersonal Psychology.

Phil has been a student of spiritual/metaphysical teachings for forty years, and has extensive knowledge of esoteric and modern spiritual wisdom and teachings, which he uses in his work with patients. He is a vast storehouse of information on such paths as Qabalah and myriad other Eastern, Western and Extradimensional teachings and his mentors have included Lisa deLongchamps, Ram Dass, Lazaris, Bashar and others. Other heroes include Sri Ramana Maharshi, Mahatma Ghandi, Colin Wilson. He has the ability to glean from and translate important concepts from the more esoteric teachers in a way that makes the wisdom as accessible as the spiritual path of 12-Step Recovery which is shared in a language that most people can grasp and progress with quite readily.

With a Masters Degree in Humanistic & Transpersonal Clinical Psychology, he is a vanguard in his field and studied with Joan

Halifax, PhD, Elisabeth Kubler-Ross, MD, Carl Rogers, PhD, Virginia Satir, Robert Hall, MD (Fritz Perl's Protégé), James Hillman, PhD, Danaan Parry and many others. Phil is also licensed Marriage & Family Therapist (CA since 1981) and certified Master Addictions Counselor. He has served as a key Staff Trainer since 2002.

Phil has lectured to audiences large and small for the past 30+ years. As a writer, Phil has been published in 'Tucson LifeLine' 1986 - 1988, 'The Sedona Journal of Emergence' 1995 - 1996, 'Addictions Professional Magazine 2004, and related publications. He has developed literature for patients that focus on specific aspects of treatment and healing. Phil's pivotal influences in literature include THE MYSTICAL QABALAH by Dion Fortune, THE MIND PARASITES by Colin Wilson, THE NATURE OF PERSONAL REALITY by Jane Roberts, WINGED PHAROAH by Joan Grant, and THE THIRD MILLENIUM by Ken Carey. Phil's interests include Sacred Geometry, Environmental Welfare, Animal Welfare, Fractals, music that lifts the Spirit, Inter-Dimensional Studies, classic motorcycles/autos and Serving the Light, and Life.

His core interest is to share gems and insights that draw people deeper into their own paths of Awakening. The breadth of his knowledge and his ability to connect millenia of teachings and sacred knowledge and draw connections to how to heal our own lives and families has helped thousands of people since 1971.

His CD, THE TECHNOLOGY OF FORGIVENESS (Copyright 1992, 1997) is available through http://www.SierraTucson.com >Store>Books/Multimedia>Miscellaneous.   Or Call 520-624-4000, ask for Bookstore.

Website: http://www.near-death.com/geometry.html

ISBN 9781620301289   Copyright 2012, Phillip S. Mitchell
$8.95 USD

~ Printed on Recycled Paper ~

NOTES

NOTES

Made in the USA
Coppell, TX
22 February 2020